MORE Sight Word Books

30 Reproducible Readers to Share at School and Home

LEVEL 2

Written by
Kimberly Jordano and Tebra Corcoran

Editor: Kim Cernek
Illustrator: Darcy Tom
Cover Illustrator: Kim Graves
Cover Photographer: Michael Jarrett
Designers: Moonhee Pak and Terri Lamadrid
Cover Designer: Moonhee Pak
Art Director: Tom Cochrane
Project Director: Carolea Williams

Table of Contents

Introduction

More Sight Word Books: Level 2 features 30 cross-curricular mini-books with fun, predictable text that you reproduce and your students personalize to make their very own set of beginning readers. Because emergent readers need frequent, intensive opportunities to practice reading strategies, including the mastery of high-frequency words called sight words, the stories in this resource give students repeated practice reading and writing over 50 color words, number words, adjectives, adverbs, and simple action verbs (see list on page 8) that most commonly appear in print.

More Sight Word Books: Level 2 provides you with ways to enhance your existing literacy program by giving students at all levels the opportunity to read and write sight words; learn about directionality

(left-to-right orientation) and tracking (one-to-one correspondence); use picture clues and word patterns to read new words; develop comprehension skills; improve fluency; expand vocabulary; and spell new words. The mini-books are also excellent tools for exploring modeled reading, shared reading, independent reading, and guided reading.

More Sight Word Books: Level 2 is the perfect complement to your regular reading program or English-as-a-second-language program. As an added bonus, you can strengthen your home–school connection by encouraging students to take home their mini-books to share with their family. This collection of sight word mini-books is sure to inspire in every student an enthusiasm for reading!

Getting Started

Choose a mini-book to use for a class lesson. Use the mini-books in sequence, or select those that fit into your current thematic unit of study. Then, adjust the challenge level of the text, if necessary (see below), and copy a set of pages for each student.

ASSEMBLING THE MINI-BOOKS AND READING STICKS

Fold each page of a mini-book backwards onto itself so that the blank side of the paper does not show. Staple the pages together in a construction paper cover so that the creased sides face out. This approach is recommended because the thick, folded pages are much easier for little fingers to turn!

Cut from construction paper or a greeting card envelope (cut widthwise) a 4" (10 cm) square for each student's mini-book. Glue to the inside front cover of each mini-book the side edges and bottom of the construction paper square or the back of the envelope to create a pocket. This pocket can hold a reading stick for students to use as they read the words in their mini-book. To make a reading stick, glue to the end of a craft stick a small object that relates to the theme of the mini-book. For example, use a sticker, an illustration cut from a bulletin board border, a student's class picture, a small plastic toy or other object (e.g., a piece of a sponge for the *Time to Wash* mini-book), or a pattern reproduced, reduced, and cut from the pattern pages (139–144). The reading sticks reinforce one-to-one correspondence and are a fun, motivational tool.

CUSTOMIZING THE CHALLENGE LEVEL

More Sight Word Books: Level 2 includes two formats to help students practice reading and writing sight words. One or two sight words have been omitted from most of the sentences in the first four mini-books of each unit. This format encourages beginning readers and writers to follow the pattern of the text to identify the missing sight word or words and then write that word or those words on the blank lines. Common sight words have been omitted from these mini-books to give students repeated practice reading and writing words that they will commonly see in print or use in their own writing. Have students use the sight words listed in the table of contents, or encourage students to write the words that they think best complete the sentences. More than one sight word has been omitted from most of the sentences in the fifth mini-book of each unit to give students an opportunity to review some of the sight words introduced in previous mini-books.

If students need a greater challenge with the mini-books, consider using liquid correction fluid or white labels to cover additional sight words in the text, draw blank lines in those places, and then make copies of the revised pages for the class.

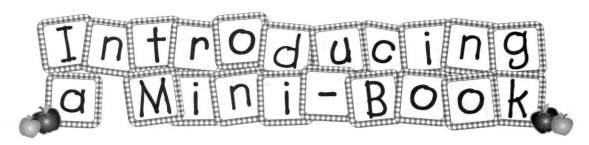

Introducing a Mini-Book

S tudents can complete their mini-books in small groups or independently at a learning center. Another option is to spend a week or so on each mini-book. Here is a sample plan.

Day One
Read aloud the book from the list of literature links on pages 9–18 that correlates with the mini-book you have chosen. Or, choose another book that matches the theme of the mini-book. Discuss the story and theme with the class.

Day Two
Copy on sentence strips the words from a mini-book. Cut apart the words, and place them in a pocket chart. Enlarge the pages of the mini-book, color and cut out the pictures, and place them above the words in the pocket chart. Read the mini-book to the class, and invite them to join you for a second reading. To extend learning, make another set of words and pictures, and give them to individual students to match to the words and pictures already in the pocket chart.

Day Three
Review the pocket chart activities from the previous day. Then, give each student an assembled mini-book (see page 4). Invite students to write their name on the first page and the name of a person to whom they would like to dedicate their book on the second page. This simple activity gives students ownership of their book and inspires them to do thoughtful work. Tell students to write the missing sight word or words (words listed in the table of contents or other words they think best complete the sentence) on the blank lines and color the pictures on each page.

Day Four
Write the title of the mini-book on each student's construction paper cover. Then, invite students to write their name on and decorate the cover of their mini-book. Or, have students cut out the title from an extra copy of the first page, glue the title to their construction paper cover, write their name on the cover, and use art supplies and/or copies of the appropriate pattern on pages 139–144 to transform the cover into an art project. For example, students can glue die-cut suns and stars to the cover of *Day and Night*, or they can color, cut out, and glue an egg copied from the Seasonal/Holiday Patterns on page 142 to the cover of *Eggs*.

Day Five
Give each student a reading stick (see page 4) that coordinates with the mini-book. Invite students to use their stick to point to the words in the mini-book as they read. Then, have students take home their mini-book to share with their family and store in their book box (see page 6).

Parent Involvement

At the beginning of the year, send home with each student a copy of the Home–School Connection Letter (page 7). This letter describes how families can use the mini-books to become more directly involved in their child's reading development. The letter also describes a book box and a sight word box that can be used to organize all of the mini-books and sight word cards.

BOOK BOX

Encourage students to practice reading their books at home with family members. A great way to keep the books organized is to store them in a personalized book box. The Home–School Connection Letter asks parents to obtain a large plastic tub with a removable lid (a shoe box is too small). Invite students to use markers, paint, and stickers to decorate their box at home. For a special touch, insert each student's name into the frame _____'s Book Box, write it on a large label, and give students their label to take home along with their copy of the parent letter.

SIGHT WORD BOX

The Home–School Connection Letter asks parents to find a recipe box or other box that is large enough to hold more than 50 index cards. For each mini-book, have students write with their parents the new sight word or words on separate index cards and add the cards to their box. Remind students to practice reading their word cards to their family members.

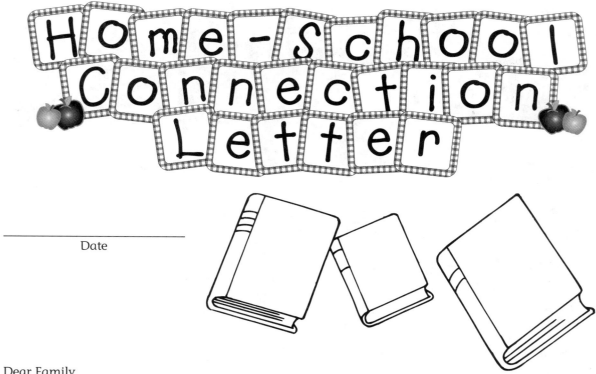

Home-School Connection Letter

_____
Date

Dear Family,

We are beginning a program that will help your child learn to read and write over 50 words that appear most frequently in books. Examples of these words are *one, say,* and *very.* Learning to read these words by sight is an important strategy your child can use to become a strong, independent reader.

Each week or two, your child will bring home a mini-book that he or she has completed in class. Please ask your child to read this book to you each night. Beginning readers need frequent opportunities to practice reading.

Your child will complete 30 mini-books this year. Please find a plastic tub with a removable lid (a shoe box is too small), and help your child decorate it. Encourage your child to use this book box to store his or her mini-books. Also, please find a recipe box or other box that is large enough to hold more than 50 index cards. Each week, write on separate index cards the sight words featured in the latest mini-book, and place the cards in the sight word box. Encourage your child to practice reading these words at home.

Together, we can teach your child beginning reading skills and inspire him or her to love books!

Sincerely,

Sight Words List

always	help	play	ten
best	hot	purple	their
big	jump	put	these
black	know	red	three
blue	little	ride	today
brown	many	said	too
carry	never	say	two
cold	new	seven	up
day	night	share	very
down	nine	sit	walk
eat	none	six	wash
eight	once	sleep	white
five	one	small	work
fly	orange	stop	yellow
four	out	take	
green	pink	tell	

Mini-Book Overviews

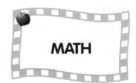

MATH

Jungle Numbers

Literature Link: *Roar! A Noisy Counting Book* by Pamela Duncan Edwards (HarperCollins)

Focus Words: number words for 1–5

Cover Art: Have students glue a paper coconut tree to their cover and then use paint markers to write numbers on their tree.

Reading Stick: Glue a paper safari hat (page 139) to a craft stick.

Cookies, Please!

Literature Link: *Cookie Count: A Tasty Pop-Up* by Robert Sabuda (Little Simon)

Focus Words: number words for 1–5

Other Sight Words: eat, up

Cover Art: Have students color paper cookies (page 139), glue raisins on them, glue the cookies to a paper plate, and glue the plate to their cover.

Reading Stick: Glue a chocolate chip or raisin to a craft stick.

My Piggy Bank

Literature Link: *Benny's Pennies* by Pat Brisson (Doubleday Books)

Focus Words: number words for 6–10

Cover Art: Have students color a paper piggy bank (page 139) and glue it to their cover.

Reading Stick: Glue a penny to a craft stick.

On the Farm

Literature Link: *One Cow Moo Moo!*
by David Bennett and Andy Cooke
(HENRY HOLT AND COMPANY)

Focus Words: number words for 6–10

Cover Art: Have students color a paper barn (page 139) and glue it to their cover.

Reading Stick: Glue a pink pom-pom to a craft stick. Then, glue pink felt ears and wiggly eyes to the pom-pom to make a "pig."

Late Again

Literature Link: *How Many How Many How Many*
by Rick Walton
(CANDLEWICK PRESS)

Focus Words: number words for 1–10

Other Sight Word: out

Cover Art: Have students color a paper clock (page 139) and glue it to their cover. Then, have them insert a metal fastener through the hands of the clock and insert the fastener through the center of the clock.

Reading Stick: Glue a paper school bus (page 143) to a craft stick.

SELF-ESTEEM

Me

Literature Link: *Quick As a Cricket*
by Audrey Wood
(CHILD'S PLAY)

Focus Word: big

Other Sight Word: small

Cover Art: Have students glue their photo on a paper square and then glue the square to their cover. Have students use dot markers to create a "frame" for their photo.

Reading Stick: Glue a small photo of each student to a craft stick.

Family

Literature Link: *Families Share*
by Rozanne Lanczak Williams
(CREATIVE TEACHING PRESS)

Focus Word: these

Other Sight Words: eat, ride, their, walk

Cover Art: Have students press their thumb in ink, stamp it several times on their cover, draw their family members' facial features on the thumbprints, and write the name of each family member below their thumbprint "people."

Reading Stick: Glue a heart sticker or a paper heart (page 140) to a craft stick.

Too Hot, Too Cold

Literature Link: *Somebody and the Three Blairs*
by Marilyn Tolhurst
(SCHOLASTIC)

Focus Word: too

Other Sight Words: cold, hot, said

Cover Art: Have students color a paper bowl (page 140), glue it to their cover, and glue dry oatmeal to the top of their bowl.

Reading Stick: Use a real plastic spoon as a reading stick.

Blue Is Best

Literature Link: *Shoes from Grandpa*
by Mem Fox
(ORCHARD BOOKS)

Focus Word: best

Other Sight Words: color words, new, say

Cover Art: Have students color a paper hat (page 140) blue and glue it to their cover.

Reading Stick: Glue a scrap of blue fabric to a craft stick.

These New Crayons

Literature Link: *The Crayon Box That Talked*
by Shaine DeRolf
(SCHOLASTIC)

Focus Words: cold, hot, new, small, these

Other Sight Words: best, big, color words

Cover Art: Have students color a paper crayon box (page 140) and glue it to their cover.

Reading Stick: Glue a real crayon to a craft stick.

SCIENCE

Is It Alive?

Literature Link: *Is It Alive?*
by Kimberlee Graves
(CREATIVE TEACHING PRESS)

Focus Word: take

Other Sight Words: know, walk

Cover Art: Have students glue a strip of sand-paper and fish crackers to a blue cover.

Reading Stick: Glue a real or paper seashell (page 141) to a craft stick.

Can You Tell?

Literature Link: *Tell Me a Season*
by Mary McKenna Siddals
(CLARION)

Focus Word: put

Other Sight Word: tell

Cover Art: Have students color a paper ther-mometer (page 141) and glue it to their cover. Then, have them draw raindrops, snowflakes, and a sun around the thermometer.

Reading Stick: Glue a cotton ball to a craft stick.

Day and Night

Literature Link: *The Very Lonely Firefly*
by Eric Carle
(PUTNAM PUBLISHING GROUP)

Focus Word: sleep

Other Sight Words: day, night, work

Cover Art: Have students glue a strip of black construction paper to the bottom half of a blue construction paper cover. Then, have students attach a yellow circle sticker to the top half of their cover and several star stickers to the bottom half of their cover.

Reading Stick: Glue a paper sun or moon (page 141) to a craft stick.

Play with Me

Literature Link: *Charlie the Caterpillar*
by Dom DeLuise
(SIMON & SCHUSTER)

Focus Word: play

Other Sight Words: fly, said, sleep

Cover Art: Have students press their thumb in ink, stamp it several times on their cover (stamping the prints side by side), and then draw facial features and legs to make a "caterpillar."

Reading Stick: Glue a butterfly sticker or a paper butterfly (page 141) to a craft stick.

Before Bed

Literature Link: *Time to Sleep*
by Denise Fleming
(SCHOLASTIC)

Focus Words: help, put, sleep

Other Sight Word: little

Cover Art: Have students glue a paper moon (page 141) to a black construction paper cover. Then, have them drip small drops of glue around the moon and sprinkle silver glitter over their cover.

Reading Stick: Glue a teddy bear sticker to a craft stick.

Boo!

Literature Link: *Boo Who?* by Joan Holub (SCHOLASTIC)

Focus Words: color words

Cover Art: Have students finger-paint a white ghost on a black construction paper cover.

Reading Stick: Glue a pumpkin sticker or a paper pumpkin (page 142) to a craft stick.

Thanksgiving

Literature Link: *Look Who's in the Thanksgiving Play!* by Andrew Clements (LITTLE SIMON)

Focus Words: color words

Other Sight Word: share

Cover Art: Have students paint their palm brown and each finger of their hand a different color and stamp their hand on their cover to make a "turkey." Then, have them draw facial features and legs on their turkey.

Reading Stick: Use a real plastic fork as a reading stick, or glue a paper fork (page 144) to a craft stick.

Just for Me

Literature Link: *I Need a Valentine!* by Harriet Ziefert (LITTLE SIMON)

Focus Words: color words

Cover Art: Have students write their name and address on a small paper rectangle, draw a stamp or place a real stamp on the rectangle, and then glue the "envelope" to their cover.

Reading Stick: Glue a 1¢ stamp to a craft stick.

Eggs

Literature Link: *Seven Eggs*
by Meredith Hooper
(HARPERCOLLINS)

Focus Words: color words

Other Sight Word: out

Cover Art: Have students color seven paper eggs (page 142) and glue them to their cover.

Reading Stick: Glue a jelly bean to a craft stick.

Holiday Fun

Literature Link: *What Is Your Language?*
by Debra Leventhal
(DUTTON)

Focus Words: color words

Cover Art: Have students use stencils to trace on holiday wrapping paper the letters of the words *Holiday Fun,* cut out the letters, and glue the letters to their cover.

Reading Stick: Glue a paper snowflake (page 142) to a craft stick.

ANIMALS

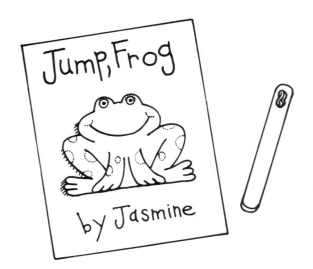

Jump, Frog

Literature Link: *Jump, Frog, Jump*
by Robert Kalan
(MULBERRY BOOKS)

Focus Word: jump

Other Sight Words: out, play

Cover Art: Have students color a paper frog (page 143) and glue it to their cover.

Reading Stick: Glue a raisin or black bean "bug" to a craft stick.

Little Ants

Literature Link: *Hey, Little Ant*
by Phillip and Hannah Hoose
(TRICYCLE PRESS)

Focus Word: carry

Other Sight Words: eat, hot, little, stop

Cover Art: Have students color a paper picnic basket (page 143), glue it to their cover, and glue black bean "ants" around the picnic basket.

Reading Stick: Glue a black bean ant to a craft stick.

Time to Wash

Literature Link: *Mrs. Wishy-Washy*
by Joy Cowley
(SHORTHAND)

Focus Word: wash

Other Sight Words: play, say, today

Cover Art: Have students glue dry laundry soap or potato flakes to a blue construction paper cover.

Reading Stick: Glue a piece of sponge or a paper scrub brush (page 143) to a craft stick.

A Ride to the Zoo

Literature Link: *Going to the Zoo*
by Tom Paxton
(MORROW JUNIOR)

Focus Word: ride

Other Sight Word: sit

Cover Art: Have students color a paper school bus (page 143) and glue it to their cover.

Reading Stick: Glue a zoo animal sticker to a craft stick.

The Rain Forest

Literature Link: *Rumble in the Jungle*
by Giles Andreae
(Tiger Tales)

Focus Words: eat, say, stop

Other Sight Words: these, walk

Cover Art: Have students press half of a potato in green paint and stamp it several times on their cover to make "leaves." Then, have them press the leafy end of a bunch of celery stalks in red paint and stamp it several times over the leaves to make "flowers."

Reading Stick: Glue a paper bunch of bananas (page 143) to a craft stick.

JUST FOR FUN

Seesaw Friends

Literature Link: *Just a Little Bit*
by Ann Tompert
(Harcourt)

Focus Words: down, up

Cover Art: Have students color a paper seesaw (page 144) and glue it to their cover.

Reading Stick: Glue a mouse sticker to a craft stick.

How Many?

Literature Link: *My Little Sister Ate One Hare*
by Bill Grossman
(Scholastic)

Focus Words: many, today

Other Sight Words: eat, none

Cover Art: Have students glue a bug sticker to a paper plate and glue the plate to their cover.

Reading Stick: Use a real plastic fork as a reading stick, or glue a paper fork (page 144) to a craft stick.

Once

Literature Link: *Froggy's First Kiss*
by Jonathan London
(SCHOLASTIC)

Focus Words: never, once

Cover Art: Have students drink a cup of red fruit punch or eat a red ice pop and then kiss a white construction paper cover to make lip prints.

Reading Stick: Glue a chocolate candy Kiss® to a craft stick.

I Do, Too!

Literature Link: *Our New Puppy*
by Isabelle Harper and Barry Moser
(THE BLUE SKY PRESS®)

Focus Words: always, too

Other Sight Words: eat, sleep, take

Cover Art: Have students paint dog's paw prints and a child's footprints on their cover.

Reading Stick: Glue a small dog treat or a paper dog bone (page 144) to a craft stick.

Who Will Help?

Literature Link: *The Little Red Hen*
by Paul Galdone
(HOUGHTON MIFFLIN)

Focus Words: help, up, very

Other Sight Word: never

Cover Art: Have students glue paper triangles to their cover. Then, have them decorate the triangles with stickers to make "party hats."

Reading Stick: Glue a small gift ornament or a paper gift (page 144) to a craft stick.

Jungle
Numbers

by

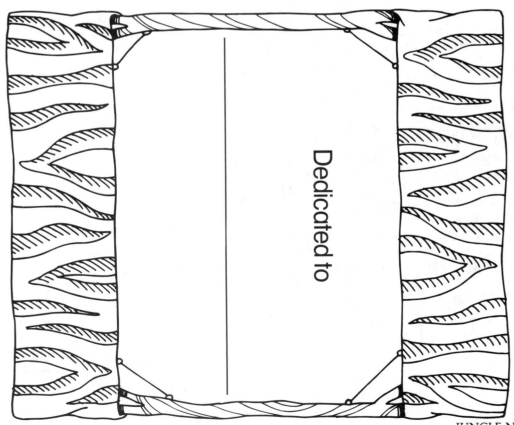

Dedicated to

More Sight Word Books: Level 2 © 2001 Creative Teaching Press

_____, _____

hippos for you.

2

_____, _____

jungle fun.

1

_____, _____,

monkeys in a tree.

3

_____ _____,

lions roar.

4

More Sight Word Books: Level 2 © 2001 Creative Teaching Press

One, _____, three,

_____, five. Now

our jungle is alive!

The End

6

_____, _____,

toucans hide.

5

More Sight Word Books: Level 2 © 2001 Creative Teaching Press

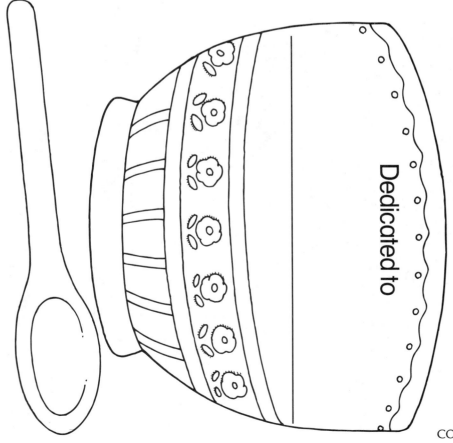

Dedicated to

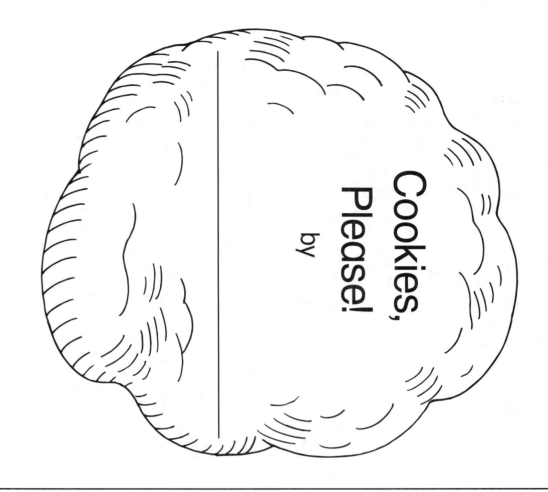

Cookies,
Please!

by

cups

——— of sugar. Stir it up.

2

egg. Stir it up.

——— 1

More Sight Word Books: Level 2 © 2001 Creative Teaching Press

_____ cups

of flour. Stir it up.

3

_____ scoops

of chocolate. Stir it up.

4

More Sight Word Books: Level 2 © 2001 Creative Teaching Press

Bake, bake, bake,

and eat them up!

The End

6

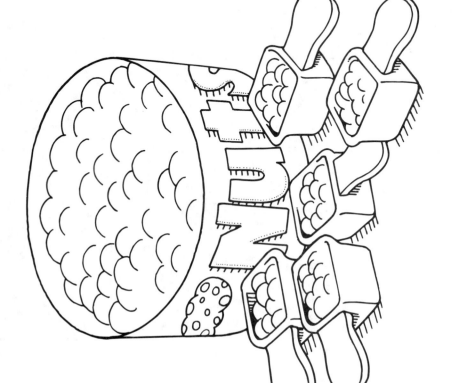

scoops

of nuts. Stir it up.

5

More Sight Word Books: Level 2 © 2001 Creative Teaching Press

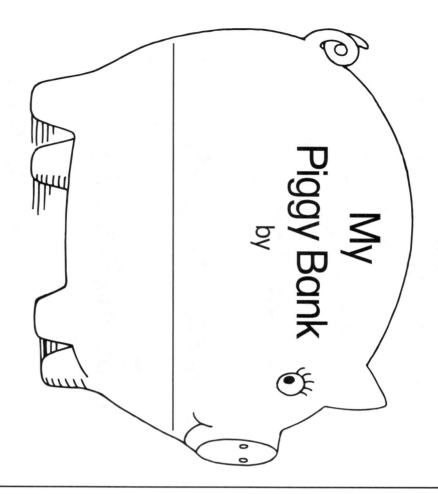

My
Piggy Bank
by

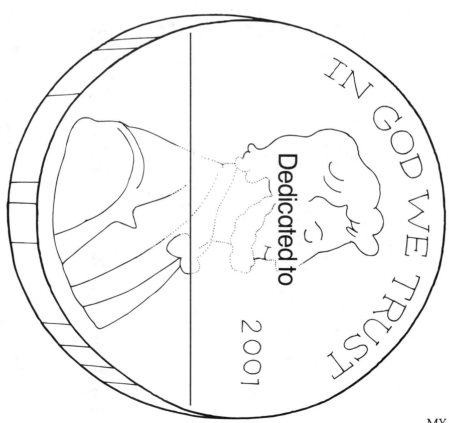

IN GOD WE TRUST

Dedicated to

2001

More Sight Word Books: Level 2 © 2001 Creative Teaching Press

_____ pennies in my piggy bank.

What will I buy with _____ pennies?

2

_____ pennies in my piggy bank. What will I buy with _____ pennies?

1

More Sight Word Books: Level 2 © 2001 Creative Teaching Press

_____ pennies in my piggy bank.

What will I buy with

_____ pennies?

3

_____ pennies in my

piggy bank. What will I buy

with

_____ pennies?

4

More Sight Word Books: Level 2 © 2001 Creative Teaching Press

Zero pennies in my piggy bank. I think I will cry!

The End

6

_____ pennies in my piggy bank. What will I buy with _____ pennies?

5

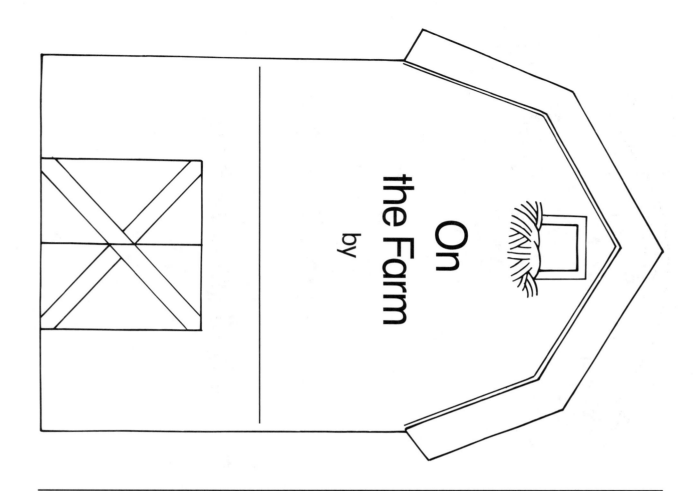

On
the Farm

by

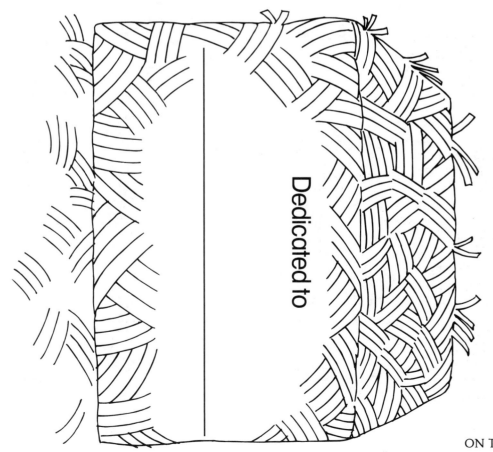

Dedicated to

Mother dog counts

her pups. Bow-wow.

_____ pups.

2

Mother hen counts

her chicks. Cluck. Cluck.

_____ chicks.

1

More Sight Word Books: Level 2 © 2001 Creative Teaching Press

Mother cat counts her

kittens. Meow. Meow.

_____ kittens.

3

Mother duck counts her

ducklings. Quack. Quack.

_____ ducklings.

4

More Sight Word Books: Level 2 © 2001 Creative Teaching Press

_____, seven,

_____, nine,

_____.

Let the farm fun begin!

The End

6

Mother pig counts

her piglets. Oink. Oink.

_____ piglets.

5

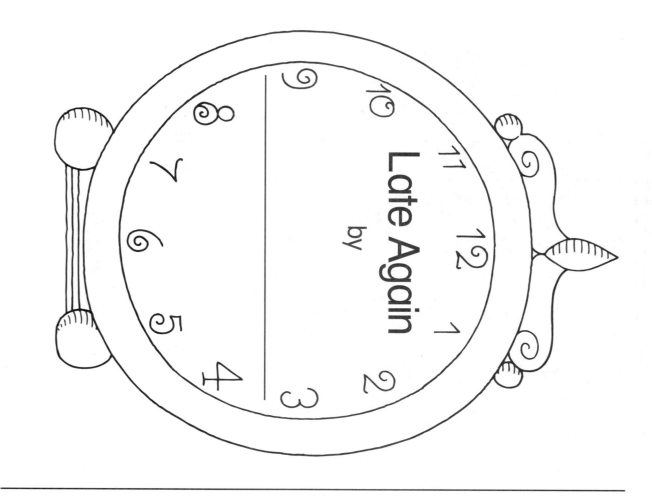

Late Again

by

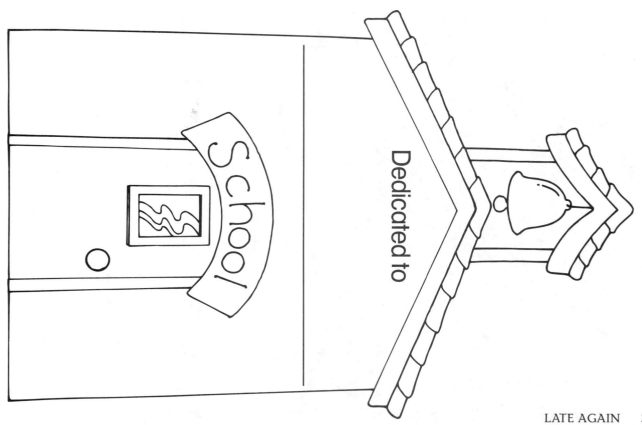

Dedicated to

More Sight Word Books: Level 2 © 2001 Creative Teaching Press

One, _____ .

Tie my shoe.

1

_____ , four.

Out the door.

2

More Sight Word Books: Level 2 © 2001 Creative Teaching Press

Kick some sticks _____, _____.

3

Don't be late _____, _____.

4

Now I'll have to walk again!

The End

6

_____, _____

Missed the bus again.

5

More Sight Word Books: Level 2 © 2001 Creative Teaching Press

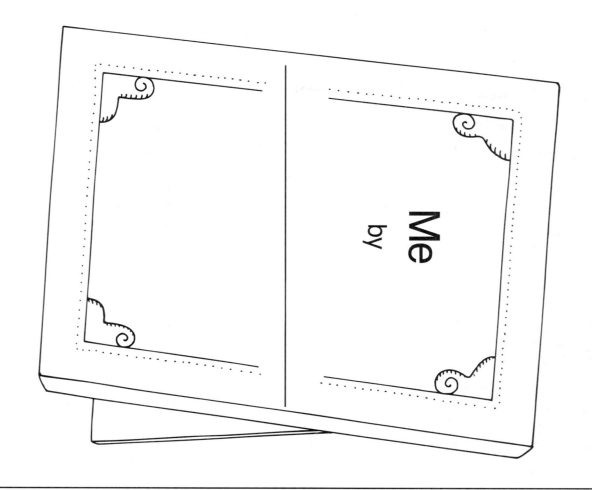

Me
by

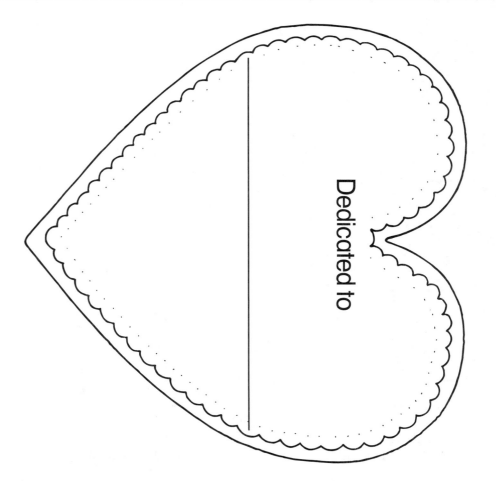

Dedicated to

I may be small, but I can

build a _____ building.

2

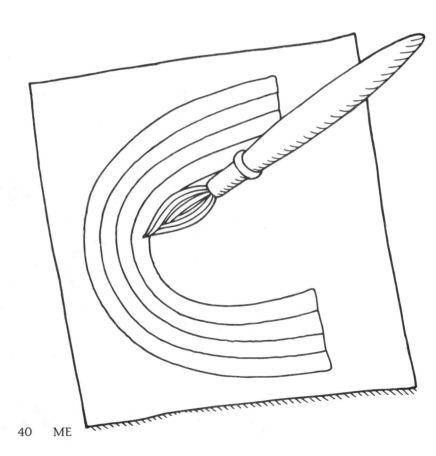

I may be small, but I can

paint a _____ picture.

1

More Sight Word Books: Level 2 © 2001 Creative Teaching Press

I may be small, but I can

make a _____

snowman.

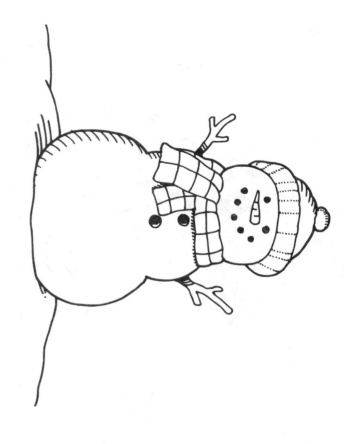

3

I may be small, but I can

make a _____

sandwich.

4

More Sight Word Books: Level 2 © 2001 Creative Teaching Press

I may be small, but I can

give a ———— hug!

The End

6

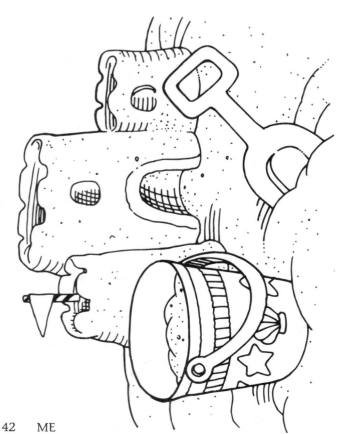

I may be small, but I can

build a ————

sand castle.

5

More Sight Word Books: Level 2 © 2001 Creative Teaching Press

Family

by

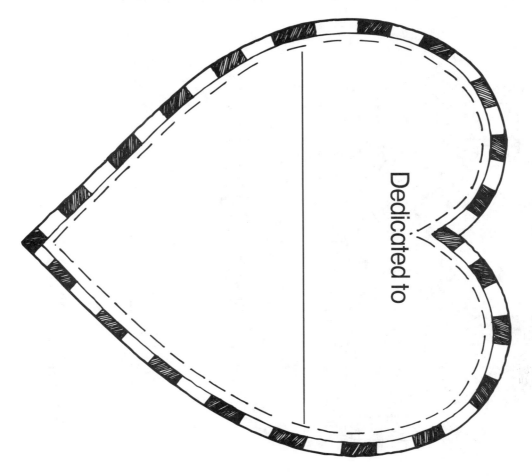

Dedicated to

people eat _____

their dinner together.

1

people walk _____

their dog together.

2

their friends together.

_____ people visit

3

their bikes together.

_____ people ride

4

They are a family!

The End

6

Who are _____

people?

5

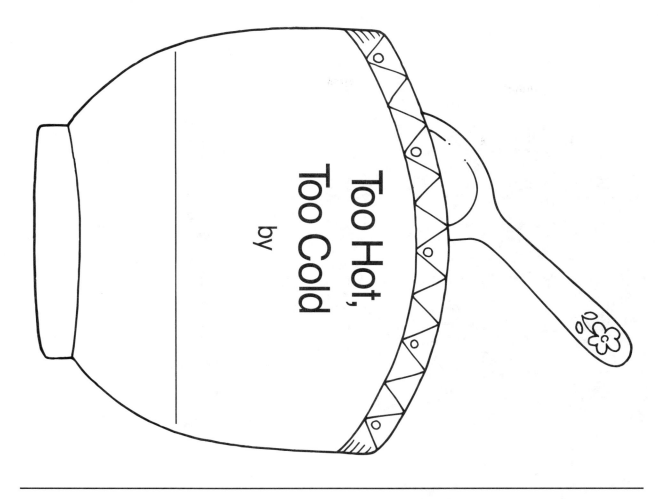

Too Hot,
Too Cold

by

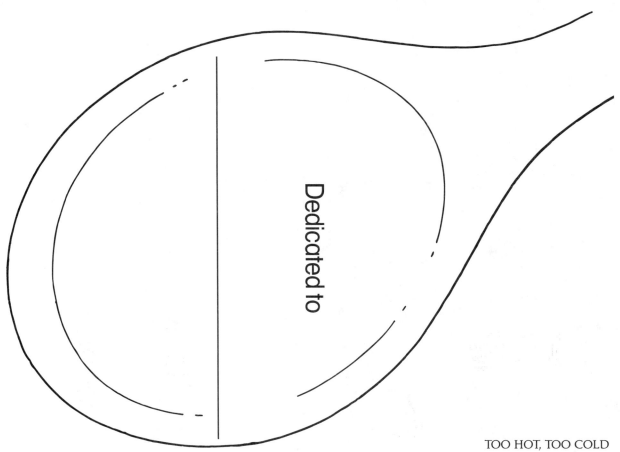

Dedicated to

"This cereal is _____

hot!" said Mama.

2

"This cereal is _____

hot!" said Papa.

1

More Sight Word Books: Level 2 © 2001 Creative Teaching Press

"This cereal is

hot!" said Baby. So they

went for a walk.

3

"This cereal is

cold!" said Papa.

4

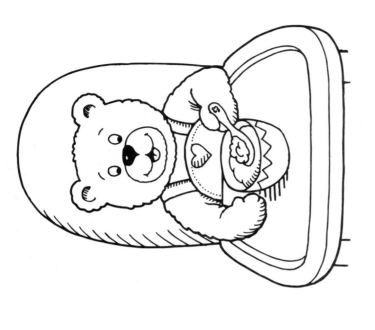

"This cereal is just right!" said

Baby. And he ate it all up!

The End

6

"This cereal is _____

cold!" said Mama.

5

More Sight Word Books: Level 2 © 2001 Creative Teaching Press

Blue
Is Best
by

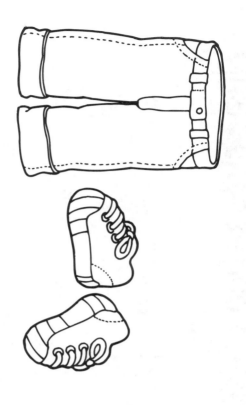

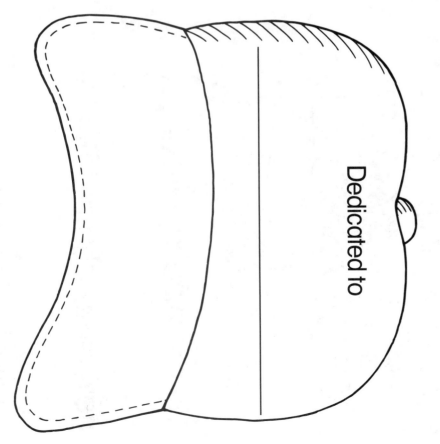

Dedicated to

More Sight Word Books: Level 2 © 2001 Creative Teaching Press

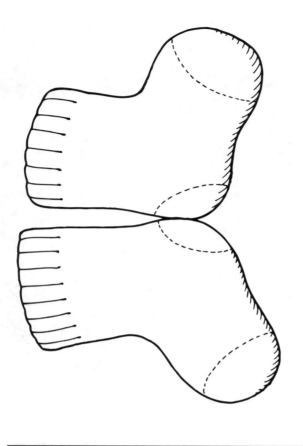

My mom says, "Wear your new orange socks." But I like my blue socks _____.

2

My mom says, "Wear your new black shoes." But I like my blue shoes _____.

1

More Sight Word Books: Level 2 © 2001 Creative Teaching Press

My mom says, "Wear your new green jeans." But I like my blue jeans _____.

3

My mom says, "Wear your new white shirt." But I like my blue shirt _____.

4

More Sight Word Books: Level 2 © 2001 Creative Teaching Press

"Hooray!" I say. "Blue is every day!"

The End

6

My mom says, "Wear your new blue baseball cap."

5

More Sight Word Books: Level 2 © 2001 Creative Teaching Press

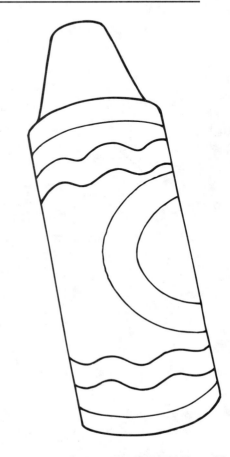

These
New Crayons

by

Dedicated to

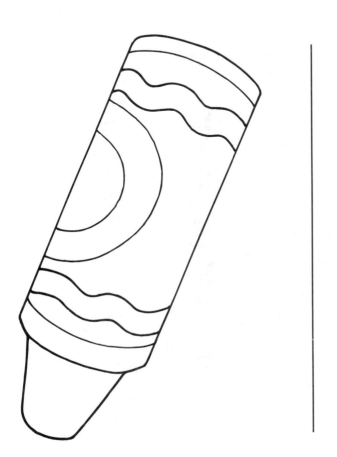

With ____

new crayons I color

____ things blue.

2

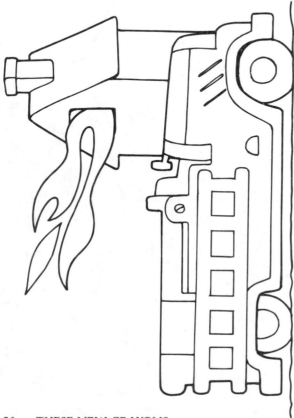

With ____

new crayons I color

____ things red.

1

More Sight Word Books: Level 2 © 2001 Creative Teaching Press

With _____ _____ crayons I color

big things black.

3

With _____ _____ new crayons I color

_____ _____ things yellow.

4

More Sight Word Books: Level 2 © 2001 Creative Teaching Press

red

blue

black

yellow

I color best with

_____ crayons!

The End

6

With _____ crayons

I color a city.

5

More Sight Word Books: Level 2 © 2001 Creative Teaching Press

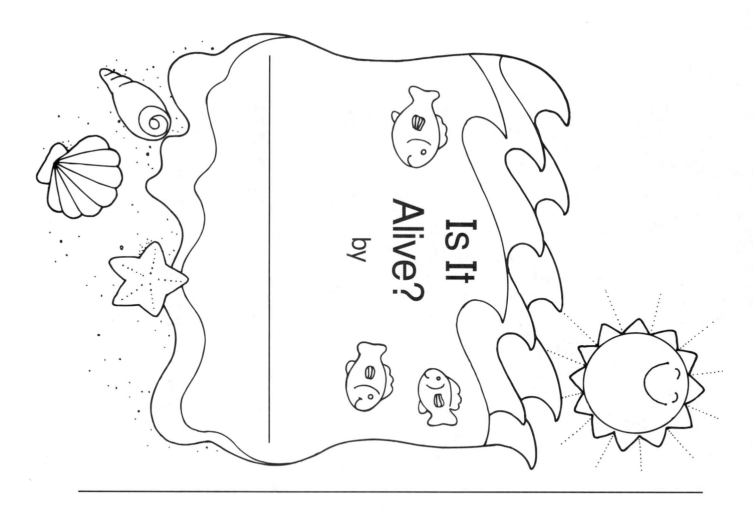

Is It
Alive?

by

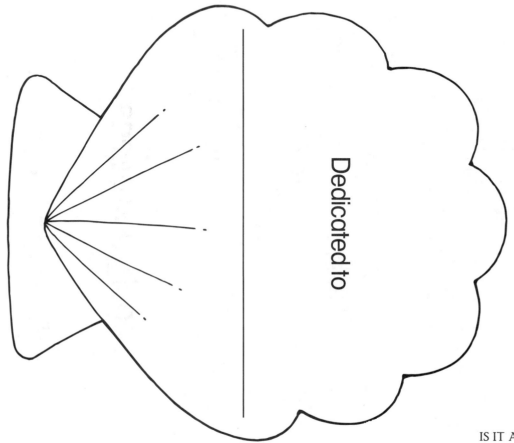

Dedicated to

I _____ a walk on

the beach, and I see a

seal. I know it is alive.

2

I _____ a walk on

the beach, and I see a

rock. I know it is not alive.

1

I _____ a walk on
the beach, and I see a
pail. I know it is not alive.

3

I _____ a walk on
the beach, and I see a
crab. I know it is alive.

4

More Sight Word Books: Level 2 © 2001 Creative Teaching Press

I _____ a walk

on the beach. I know

I am alive. Splash!

The End

6

I _____ a walk on

the beach, and I see a

boat. I know it is not alive.

5

More Sight Word Books: Level 2 © 2001 Creative Teaching Press

Can
You Tell?

by

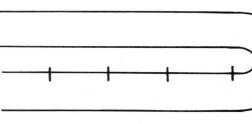

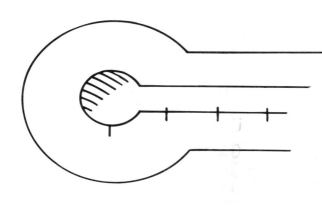

Dedicated to

More Sight Word Books: Level 2 © 2001 Creative Teaching Press

How can you tell it is spring?

I _____ on my shorts.

2

How can you tell it is winter?

I _____ on my jacket.

1

More Sight Word Books: Level 2 © 2001 Creative Teaching Press

How can you tell it is

summer? I _____

on my bathing suit.

3

How can you tell it is fall?

I _____ on my sweater.

4

More Sight Word Books: Level 2 © 2001 Creative Teaching Press

The clothes you

on tell you all!

The End

6

How can you tell if it is winter,

spring, summer, or fall?

5

More Sight Word Books: Level 2 © 2001 Creative Teaching Press

Day
and Night

by

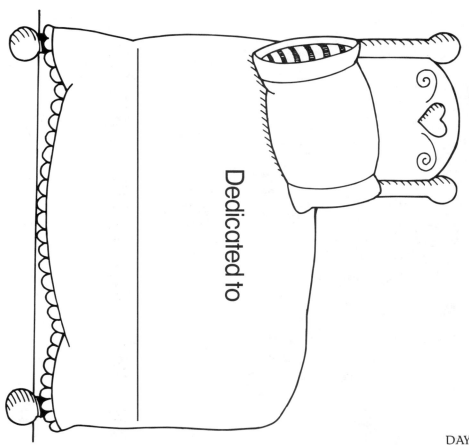

Dedicated to

A ladybug will work all day. It
_____ all night.
will

2

An owl will work all night. It
_____ all day.
will

1

More Sight Word Books: Level 2 © 2001 Creative Teaching Press

A bat will work all night. It

will _____ _____ all day.

3

A squirrel will work all day. It

will _____ _____ all night.

4

I will work all day. I will _____ all night.

The End

6

A cricket will work all night. It _____ all day.

will _____

5

Play
with Me
by

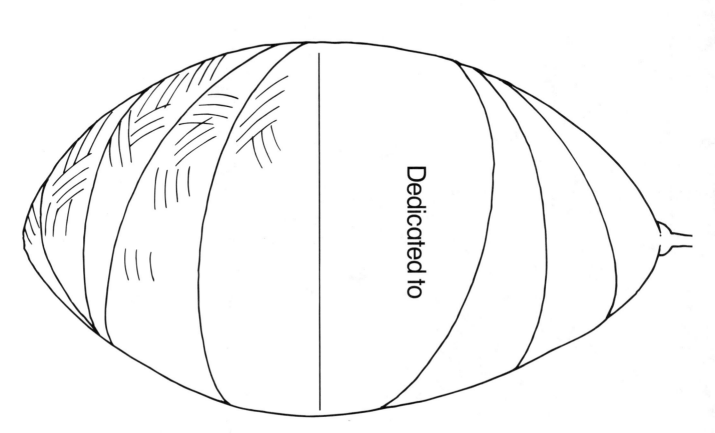

Dedicated to

"Fly over here and
_____ with me,"

said the frog.

2

"Fly over here and
_____ with me,"

said the rabbit.

1

"Fly over here and

_____ with me,"

said the turtle.

3

"Fly over here and

_____ with me,"

said the lizard.

4

More Sight Word Books: Level 2 © 2001 Creative Teaching Press

"Now I can fly over and

with you!"

The End

6

"Let me spin my chrysalis

and sleep in it," said the

caterpillar.

5

More Sight Word Books: Level 2 © 2001 Creative Teaching Press

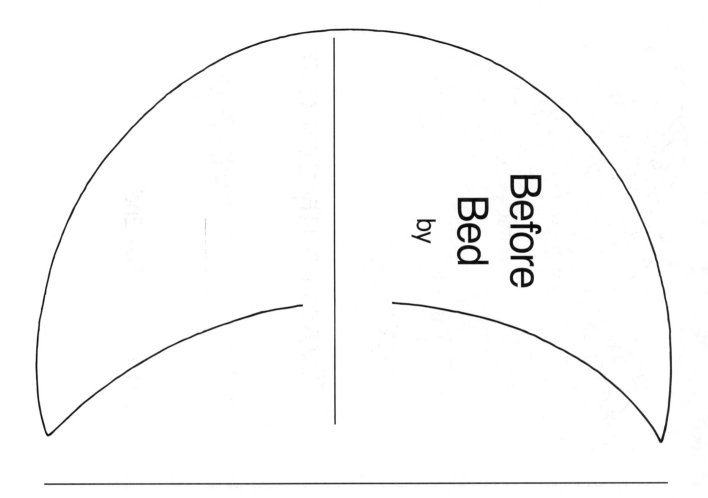

Before
Bed

by

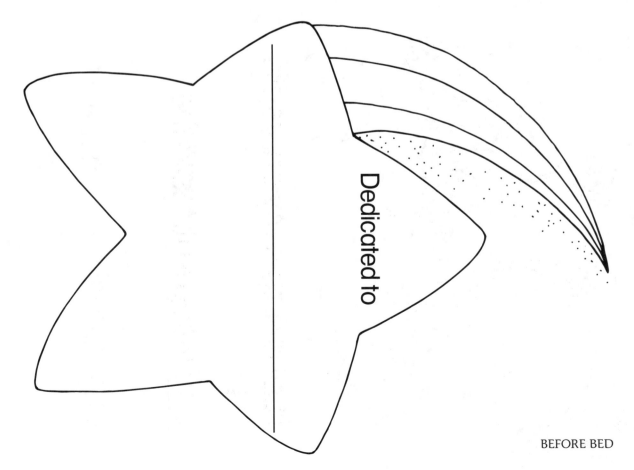

Dedicated to

Little bear will _____

gather berries before

it will sleep in the cave.

2

Little squirrel will

_____ gather nuts

before it will sleep in the tree.

1

Little bee will

_____

gather pollen before it will

in the hive.

3

Little beaver will

_____

gather logs before it will

in the lodge.

4

More Sight Word Books: Level 2 © 2001 Creative Teaching Press

will

Little

gather toys and

them away before going

to bed!

The End

6

Little rabbit will

gather carrots before it will

in the burrow.

5

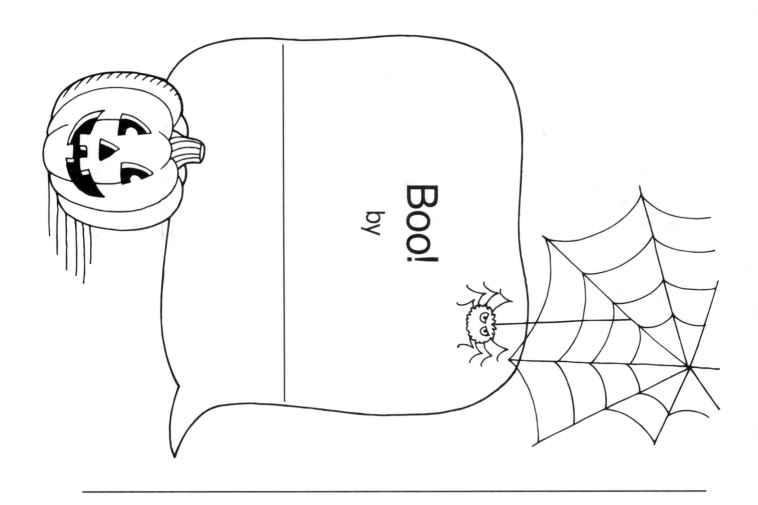

Boo!
by

Dedicated to

TRICK-OR-TREAT

More Sight Word Books: Level 2 © 2001 Creative Teaching Press

The _____ and

yellow lion says, "BOO!"

2

The _____ and

white vampire says, "BOO!"

1

More Sight Word Books: Level 2 © 2001 Creative Teaching Press

The

_____ and

green jack-o'-lantern

says, "BOO!"

3

The

_____ and

red superhero says, "BOO!"

4

More Sight Word Books: Level 2 © 2001 Creative Teaching Press

, the
_____

trick-or-treater, says, "BOO!"

The End

6

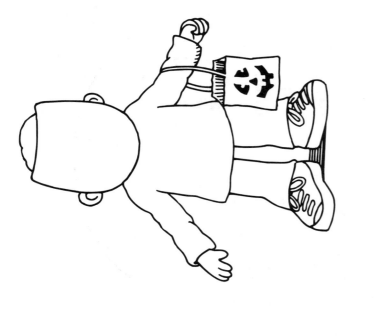

The _____ and

black monster says, "BOO!"

5

More Sight Word Books: Level 2 © 2001 Creative Teaching Press

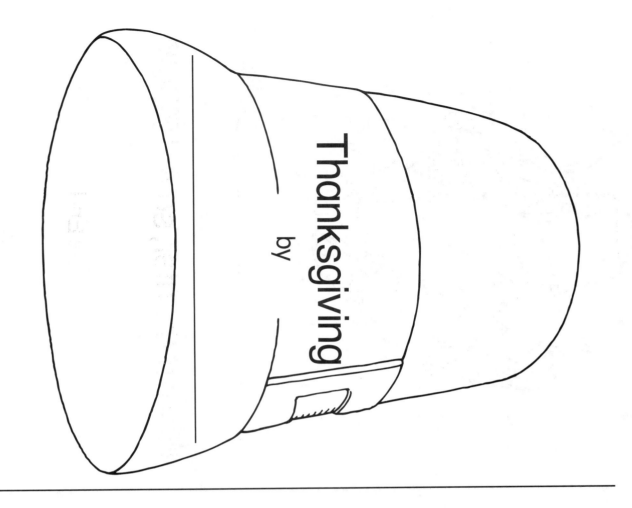

Thanksgiving

by _____

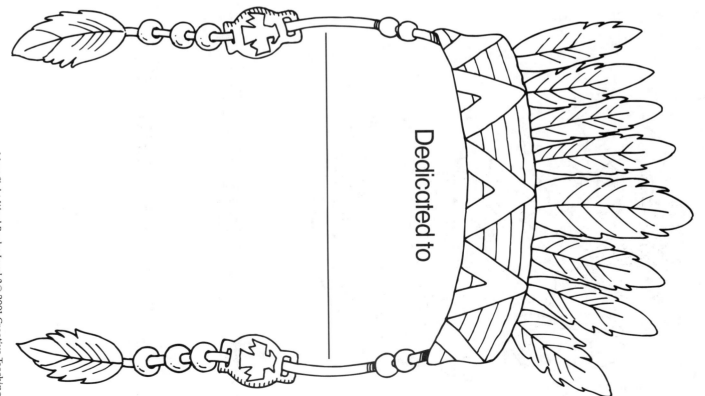

Dedicated to _____

Native Americans can share

_____ corn.

2

Pilgrims can share

_____ berries.

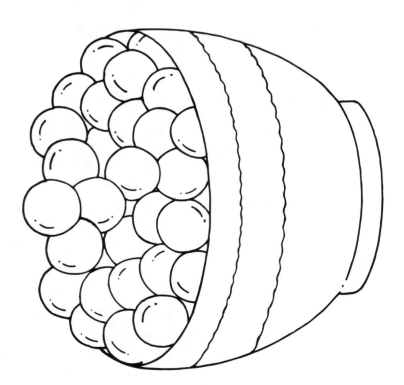

1

More Sight Word Books: Level 2 © 2001 Creative Teaching Press

Pilgrims can share an

_____
pumpkin pie.

3

Native Americans can share

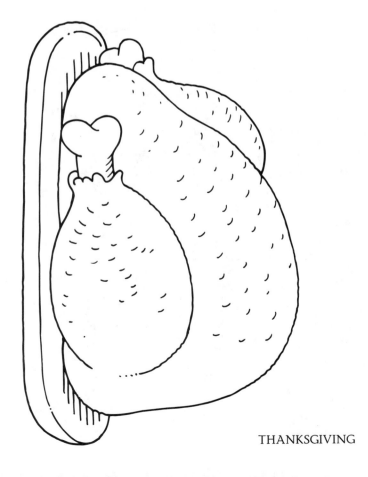

a _____ turkey.

4

More Sight Word Books: Level 2 © 2001 Creative Teaching Press

Pilgrims and Native

Americans can share

a colorful Thanksgiving!

The End

6

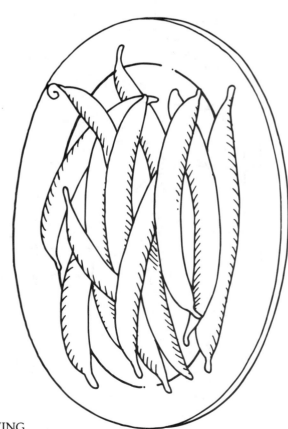

Pilgrims can share

_____ beans.

5

Just
for Me
by

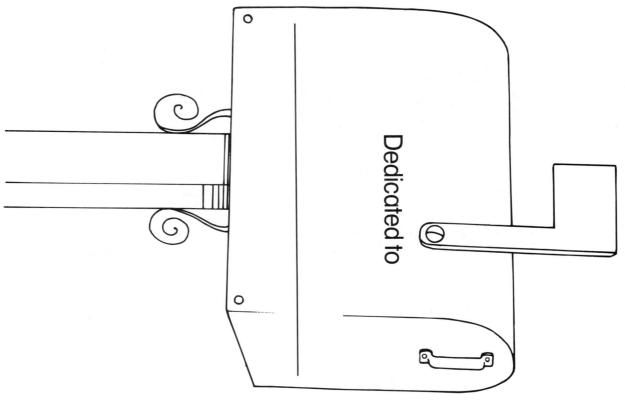

Dedicated to

A _____ and pink

heart valentine just for me.

2

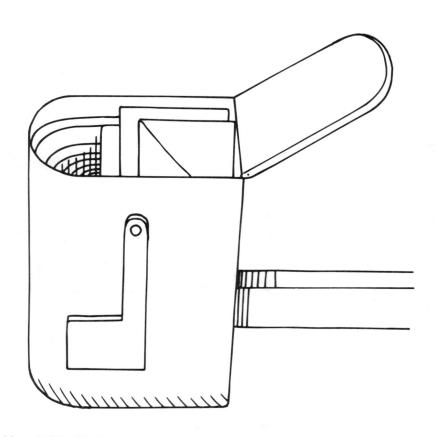

I looked in the mail.

What did I see?

1

More Sight Word Books: Level 2 © 2001 Creative Teaching Press

A _____ and white

penguin valentine just for me.

3

A _____ and

green superhero valentine

just for me.

4

More Sight Word Books: Level 2 © 2001 Creative Teaching Press

A colorful valentine present!

What could it be?

The End

6

chocolate

A _____

valentine just for me.

5

More Sight Word Books: Level 2 © 2001 Creative Teaching Press

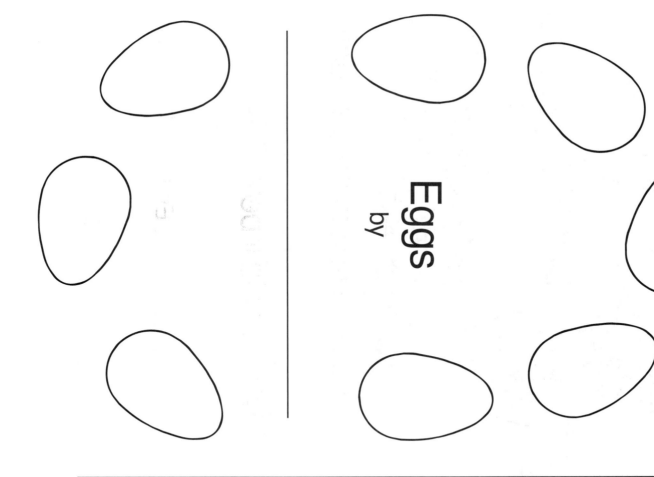

Eggs
by

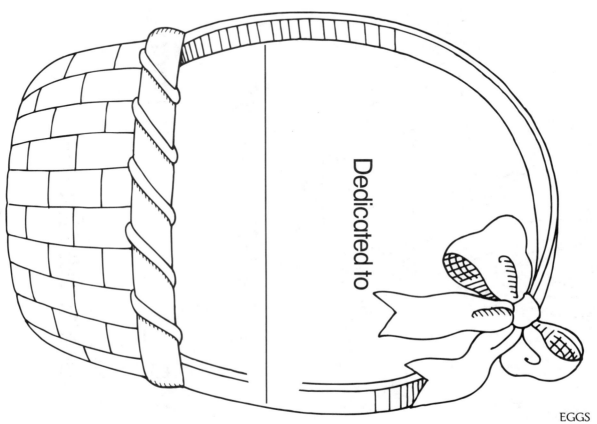

Dedicated to

On Tuesday, out came a

_____ crocodile.

2

On Monday, out came

a _____ and

white penguin.

1

More Sight Word Books: Level 2 © 2001 Creative Teaching Press

On Wednesday, out

came a brown and

_____ ostrich.

3

On Thursday, out came

a _____ lizard.

4

On Saturday and Sunday,

out came chocolate eggs!

The End

6

On Friday, out came

a _____ and

black snake.

5

More Sight Word Books: Level 2 © 2001 Creative Teaching Press

Holiday Fun

by

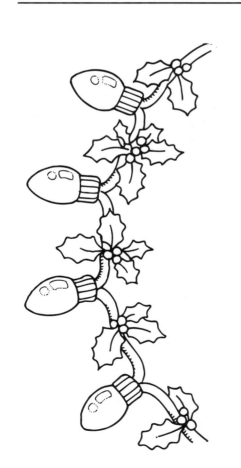

Dedicated to

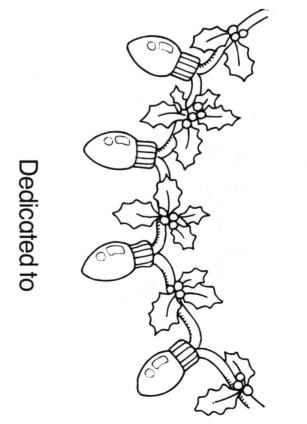

A yellow and _____

dreidel from Israel.

2

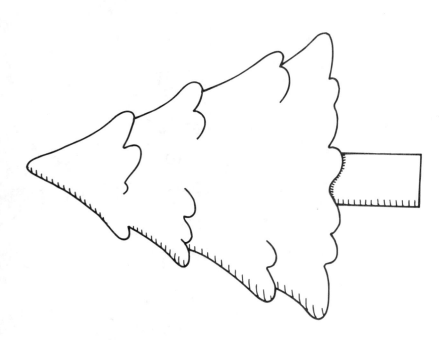

A brown and _____

Tannenbaum from Germany.

1

More Sight Word Books: Level 2 © 2001 Creative Teaching Press

A pink and

piñata from Mexico.

3

A purple and

candle from Africa.

4

More Sight Word Books: Level 2 © 2001 Creative Teaching Press

Holiday fun for everyone!

The End

6

A white and _____

Santa from the U.S.A.

5

More Sight Word Books: Level 2 © 2001 Creative Teaching Press

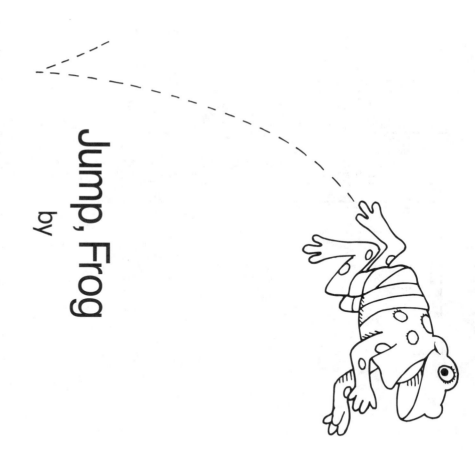

Jump, Frog

by

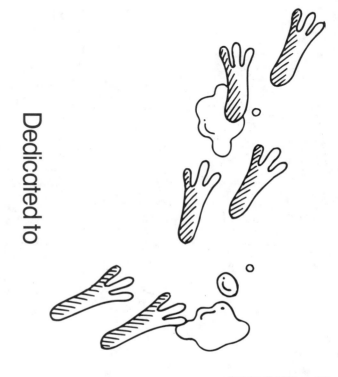

Dedicated to

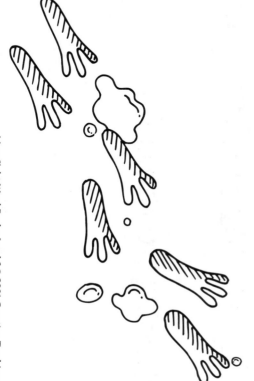

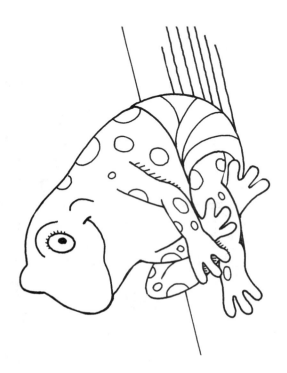

_____, frog, and
play out the door.

2

_____, frog, and
play on the floor.

1

_____, frog, and

play on the rocks.

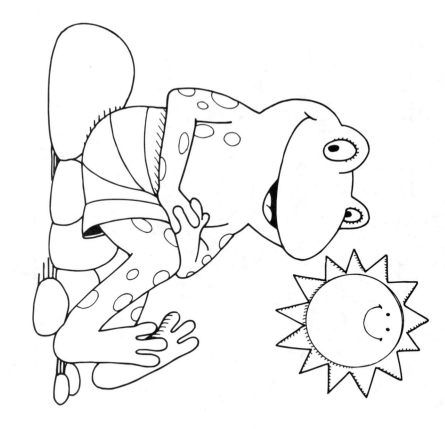

3

_____, frog, and

play in the box.

4

More Sight Word Books: Level 2 © 2001 Creative Teaching Press

_____, frog, and

play with me!

The End

6

_____, frog, and

play by the tree.

5

Little Ants

by

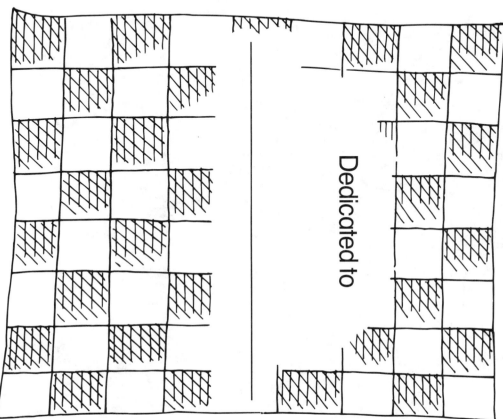

Dedicated to

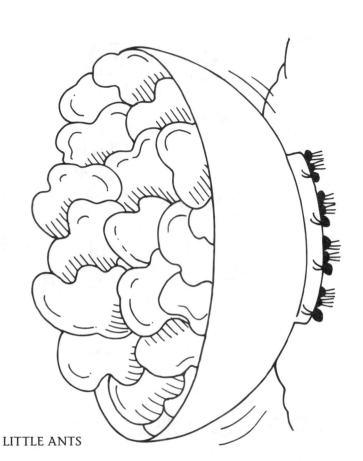

Don't stop, little ants.

———— the hot dog.

2

———

Don't stop, little ants.

———— the chips.

1

More Sight Word Books: Level 2 © 2001 Creative Teaching Press

Don't stop, little ants.

_____ the cookies.

3

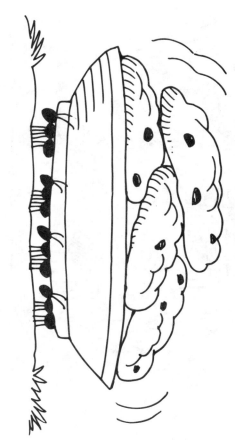

Don't stop, little ants.

_____ the pickles.

4

More Sight Word Books: Level 2 © 2001 Creative Teaching Press

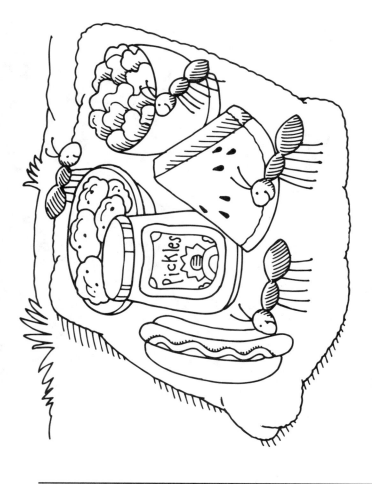

Stop, little ants! It's time to

eat your picnic treat!

The End

6

Don't stop, little ants.

the watermelon.

5

More Sight Word Books: Level 2 © 2001 Creative Teaching Press

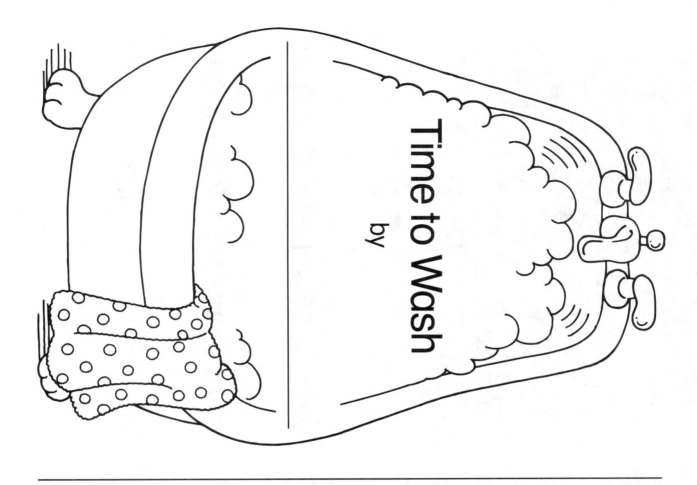

Time to Wash

by

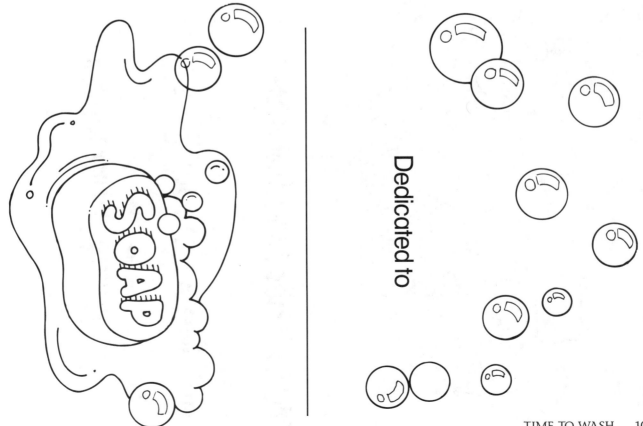

Dedicated to

Did you hear mother dog

say, "Bow-wow"? It's time

to _____ her puppies.

2

Did you hear mother cat

say, "Meow, meow"? It's time

to _____ her kittens.

1

More Sight Word Books: Level 2 © 2001 Creative Teaching Press

Did you hear mother mouse

say, "Eek, eek"? It's time to

_____ her baby mice.

3

Did you hear mother hamster

say, "Squeak, squeak"? It's

time to _____ her

baby hamsters.

4

Did you hear mother bird say,

"Chirp, chirp"? It's time to

_____ her baby birds.

5

Did you hear

mother today? It's time to

_____ 's

_____ , splash, and play!

The End

6

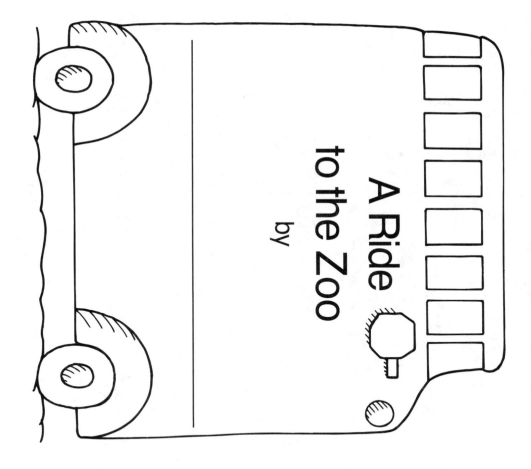

A Ride
to the Zoo
by

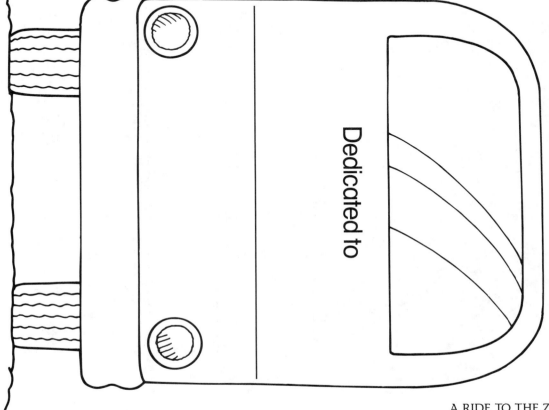

Dedicated to

I sit on the bus and _____ to the zoo.

I wonder what the giraffes will do.

2

I sit on the bus and _____ to the zoo.

I wonder what the elephants will do.

1

More Sight Word Books: Level 2 © 2001 Creative Teaching Press

I sit on the bus and

_____ to the zoo.

I wonder what the

monkeys will do.

3

I sit on the bus and

_____ to the zoo.

I wonder what the

lions will do.

4

More Sight Word Books: Level 2 © 2001 Creative Teaching Press

How much longer is this _____ to the zoo? I can't wait to see what the animals will do!

The End

6

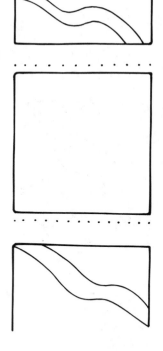

I sit on the bus and _____ to the zoo. I wonder what the snakes will do.

5

The
Rain Forest

by

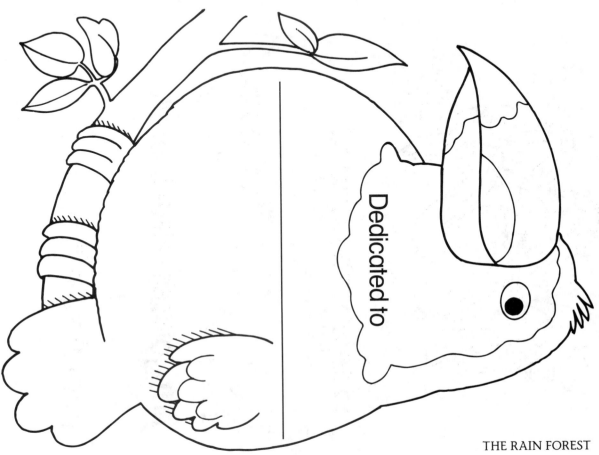

Dedicated to

I will stop and say to any

boa constrictor I see,

"Hungry snake, please don't

_____ me!"

2

I'm going to take a walk

through the rain forest.

1

I will _____ and say to any gorilla I see, "Hungry ape, please don't _____ me!"

3

I will stop and _____ to any jaguar I see, "Hungry cat, please don't _____ me!"

4

I will _____ and say

to any crocodile I see,

"Hungry croc, please don't

_____ me!"

5

I will stop and _____ to

any animal I see, "All these

fruits taste better than me!"

The End

6

More Sight Word Books: Level 2 © 2001 Creative Teaching Press

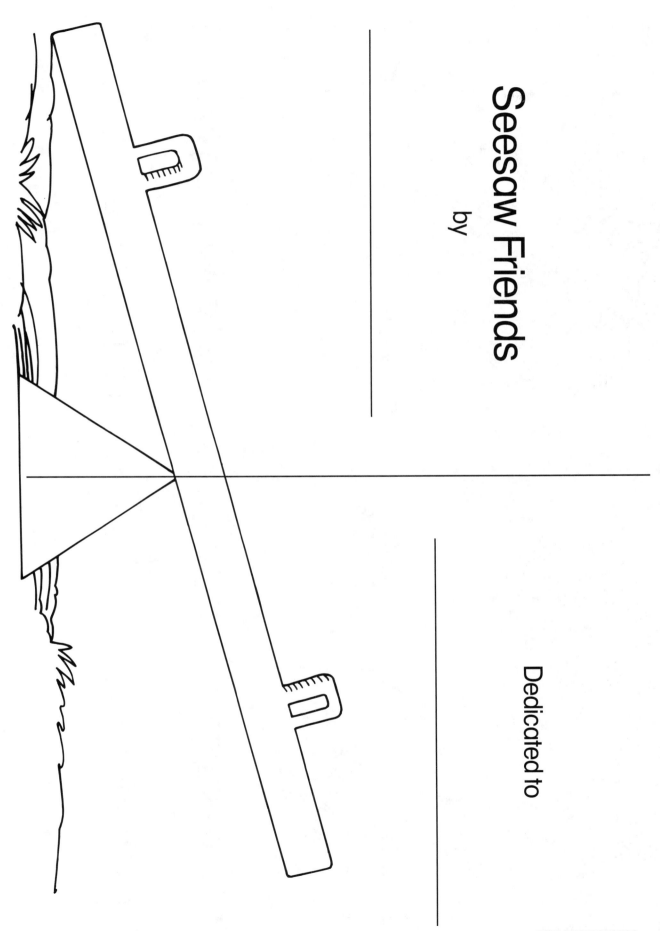

Seesaw Friends

by

_____

Dedicated to

_____

More Sight Word Books: Level 2 © 2001 Creative Teaching Press

The heavy lion touches

the ground.

2

The mouse goes _____.

The lion goes _____.

1

More Sight Word Books: Level 2 © 2001 Creative Teaching Press

The snake goes _____ .

The hippo goes

3

The heavy hippo touches

the ground.

4

More Sight Word Books: Level 2 © 2001 Creative Teaching Press

Lighter, heavier,

and _____ .

The End

6

What goes _____

must come _____ .

5

More Sight Word Books: Level 2 © 2001 Creative Teaching Press

How Many?

by

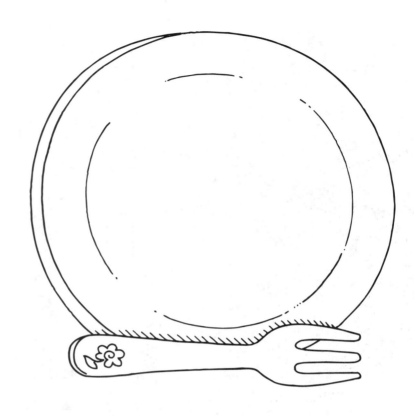

Dedicated to

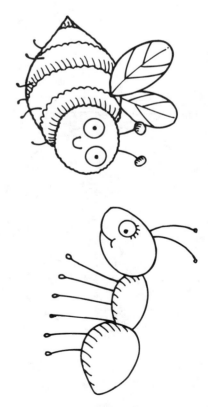

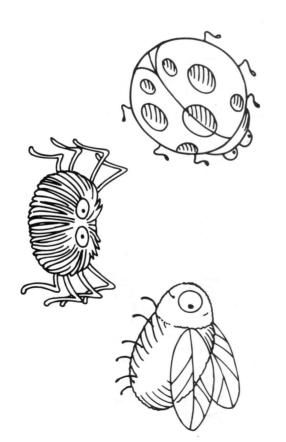

How _____

bees would you like

to eat _____ ?

None, thank you.

2

How _____

spiders would you like to

eat _____ ?

None, thank you.

1

How _____

flies would you like to

eat _____?

None, thank you.

3

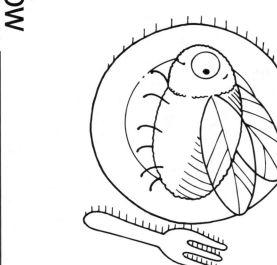

How _____

ants would you like to eat

_____?

None, thank you.

4

More Sight Word Books: Level 2 © 2001 Creative Teaching Press

How _____

cookies would you like

to eat _____, thank you.

The End

6

How _____

ladybugs would you like to

eat _____?

None, thank you.

5

More Sight Word Books: Level 2 © 2001 Creative Teaching Press

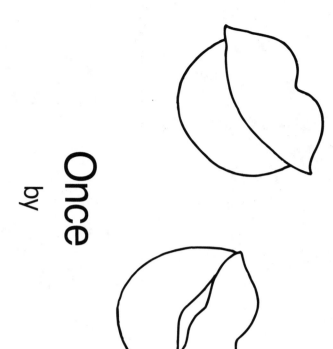

Once

by

Dedicated to

I kissed a bat.

2

I kissed a cat.

1

More Sight Word Books: Level 2 © 2001 Creative Teaching Press

But I will

kiss a rat!

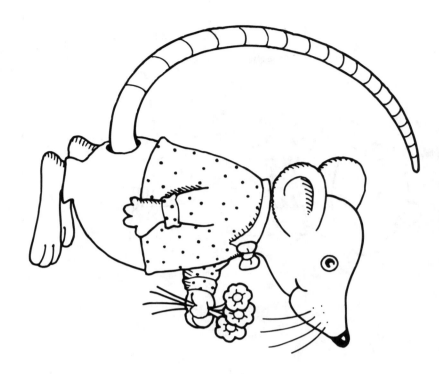

3

I kissed a hog.

4

But I will

kiss a frog!

The End

6

I kissed a dog.

5

More Sight Word Books: Level 2 © 2001 Creative Teaching Press

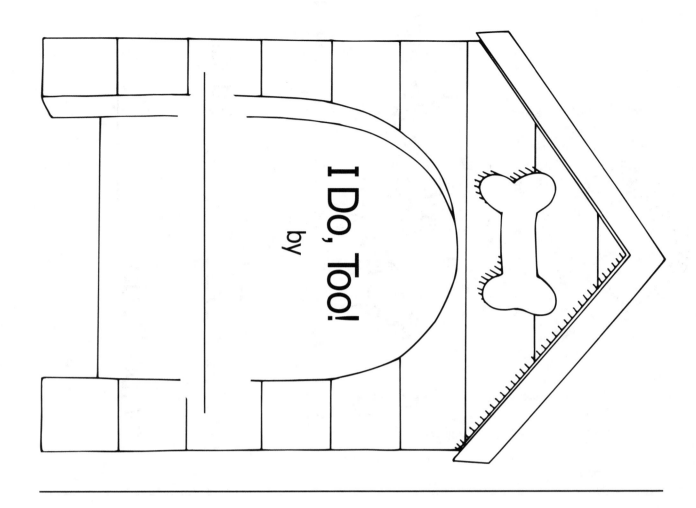

I Do, Too!
by

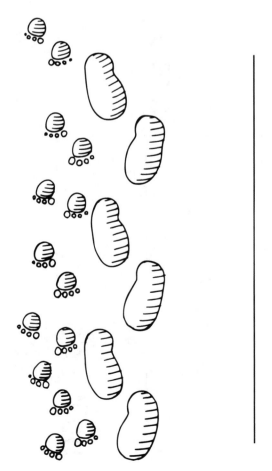

Dedicated to

More Sight Word Books: Level 2 © 2001 Creative Teaching Press

I _____ take a

bath. I do, _____ .

1

I _____ eat all

my food. I do, _____ .

2

More Sight Word Books: Level 2 © 2001 Creative Teaching Press

I _____ get wet

in the rain. I do, _____ .

3

I _____ leave

tracks. I do, _____ .

4

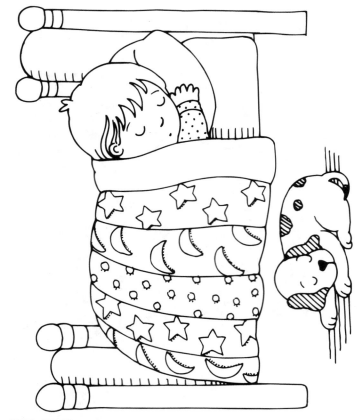

I _____ sleep

at night. I do, _____ .

5

I _____

love to be with you.

I do, _____ !

The End

6

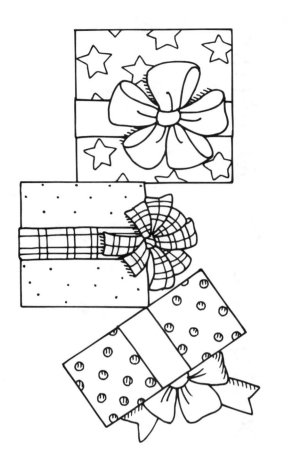

Who Will Help?

by

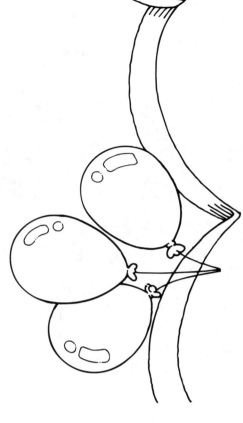

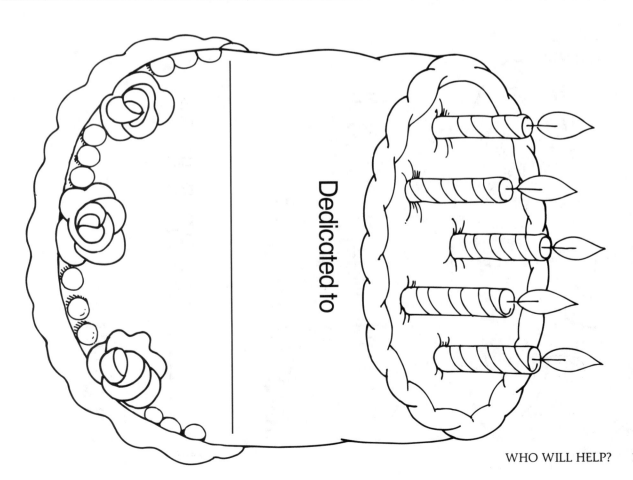

Dedicated to

"Who will help me go to the store?" "Not me! I am _____ busy," said _____ the piglet.

"Who will _____ me bake a cake?" "Not me! I am _____ busy," said the calf.

More Sight Word Books: Level 2 © 2001 Creative Teaching Press

"Who will help me blow

_____ the balloons?"

"Not me! I am _____

busy," said the lamb.

3

"Who will _____ me

wrap the presents?"

"Not me! I am _____

busy," said the duckling.

4

"Who will help me celebrate

my birthday?" "I will," said

. "I am never

too busy for you!"

The End

6

"Who will _____ me

light the candles?"

"Not me! I am _____

busy," said the kitten.

5

Math Patterns

Self-Esteem Patterns

Science Patterns

Seasonal/Holiday Patterns

More Sight Word Books: Level 2 © 2001 Creative Teaching Press

Animal Patterns

Just for Fun Patterns

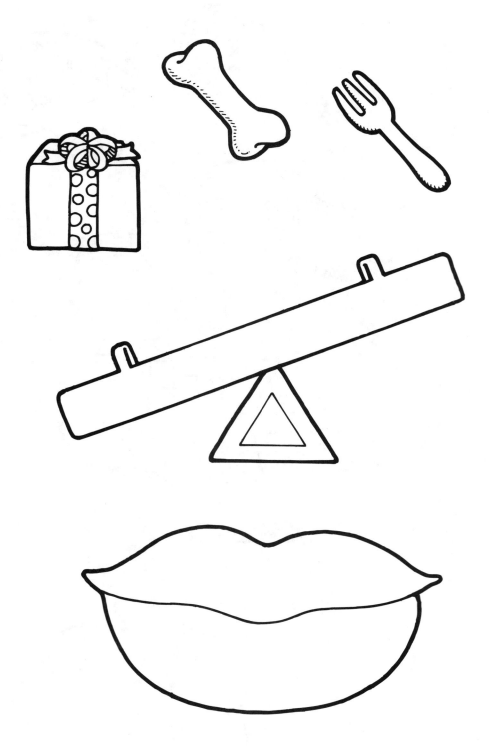

More Sight Word Books: Level 2 © 2001 Creative Teaching Press